Tulip Fever

Tulip Fever

Poems by

Lori Lamothe

© 2022 Lori Lamothe. All rights reserved.
This material may not be reproduced in any form, published,
reprinted, recorded, performed, broadcast,
rewritten or redistributed without
the explicit permission of Lori Lamothe.
All such actions are strictly prohibited by law.

Cover design by Shay Culligan
Cover image by Jan Davidsz de Heem

ISBN: 978-1-63980-171-8

Kelsay Books
502 South 1040 East, A-119
American Fork, Utah 84003
Kelsaybooks.com

for my mother

and

*To David Wyman
(1960–2022)*

*He was a man, take him for all in all,
 I shall not look upon his like again.*
                              —William Shakespeare

Acknowledgments

I am grateful to the editors of the following publications in which these poems previously appeared, sometimes in slightly different form. I would also like to thank *Gingerbread House* for nominating "A Maid at the New Yorker Cleans Room 3327" for a Pushcart Prize.

Barren Magazine: "Off US Highway 25, N."

Bird's Thumb: "Climate Cubism"

Blue River Review: "Radium Girls"

Cider Press Review: "Before Further Testing"

Common Ground Review: "The Unusual Suspects"

Del Sol Review: "Learning to Knit During a Pandemic," "Cancer Center: Key," "Future Shock"

DMQ Review: "Portrait of a Lady"

Door Is A Jar: "Chandeliers & Red Velvet"

Failbetter: "Wintering"

Gingerbread House: "Ritual," "A Maid at the New Yorker Cleans Room 3327"

Glass: A Journal of Poetry: "Garden Path with Chickens," "The Blue Tree," "Find"

Glassworks: "The Daisies"

Green Hills Literary Lantern: "Black Dog"

Honey & Lime: "Cottage Road"

Ilanot Review: "Dear Egg," "Dear Lamp"

Illumination: "Sun & All"

IthacaLit: "Poppy"

Jet Fuel Review: "Glassmaker's Travel Diary"

Kettle Blue Review: "Transport"

The Lark: "Poet vs. Novelist"

Memorious: "What the World Really Feels Like"

Menacing Hedge: "Girl in a Bee Dress," "The Cloud Sisters," "Fourth of July"

Mud Season Review: "Dragon"

Packingtown Review: "Rose-Colored Sunglasses," "The Scars"

Parhelion: "Pigeons"

Pif Magazine: "Blue Jays," "In Defense of Partiality"

Pine Hills Review: "13 Ways of Looking at an Allison"

Plath Poetry Project: "Burning the Desk"

Poets Reading the News: "Prelude"

Press 53: "The Dappled Horses of Pech-Merle"

Radioactive Moat: "American Primitive"

Red Rock Review: "Wounded Deer"

Righthand Pointing: "The Skirt"

Rogue Agent: "Post Chemo"

Scrittura: "The Dream Pilot," "Terra Incognita," "Museum of an Untrained Artist"

Shot-Glass Journal: "Somewhere Not Here"

The Shore: "Revolution in the Back Bay"

Show Us Your Papers (Main Street Rag, 2020): "Castle Rock"

Storymaker: "Red Barn in Snow," "After a Storm"

What Rough Beast: "Star Trek Power Ballad," "Palmyra"

Wicked Alice: "Breathing Lessons"

Wordgathering: "Carousel," "Bat Boy"

ZiN Daily: "At the American Philosophical Society in the City of Brotherly Love"

Contents

I Girl in a Bee Dress

    Still Life with Cheeses, Artichoke and Cherries   19
    Carousel   20
    Cottage Road   21
    The Dappled Horses of Pech-Merle   22
    Girl in a Bee Dress   23
    Bat Boy   24
    Poppy   25
    American Primitive   26
    Find   27
    After a Storm   28
    Flight   29
    At the Moulin Rouge   30
    A Maid at the New Yorker Cleans Room 3327   31
    13 Ways of Looking at an Allison   32
    Ghost   36
    The Dream Pilot   38
    Photographic Survey, 1919   39
    Monet at the Louvre   40
    The Scars   41
    Breathing Lessons   42

II Fierce Mythologies

    Revolution in the Back Bay   45
    Fourth of July   46

Transport	47
American Girls	48
Before Further Testing	49
Cancer Center: Key	50
Dragon	52
Radium Girls	53
What the World Really Feels Like	55
Pygmalion 2.0	56
Nightmare	57
The Cloud Sisters	58
Urban Decay as Latex Paint Color Palette	59
Castle Rock	60
Closed & Open Spaces	61
Names	62
Blue Nude	64
Surveillance Capitalism as Lady's Companion	65
Portrait of a Lady	66
Signs in Winter	68
Pigeons	69
Black Dog	71

III Peace Roses

Rose-Colored Sunglasses	75
The Unusual Suspects	76
The City	77

Cancer Center	78
Prelude	79
Wintering	80
The Blue Tree	81
Peace Roses	82
Dear Lamp	83
Dear Egg	84
Color in February	85
Palmyra	86
In Defense of Partiality	87
On the Drive Home	88
Terra Incognita	89
Glassmaker's Travel Diary	90
Poet vs. Novelist	91
Star Trek Power Ballad	92
Blue Jays	93
Garden Path with Chickens	94
The Skirt	95
Red Barn in Snow	96

IV Two Mirrors

Tulip Fever	99
Future Shock	101
Post Chemo	102
Self Portrait as the Allegory of Painting	103

Museum of an Untrained Artist	104
At the American Philosophical Society in the City of Brotherly Love	105
Off US Highway 25, N.	106
Climate Cubism	107
At the Solstice	108
Chandeliers & Red Velvet	109
Burning the Desk	110
Ritual	112
Learning to Knit During a Pandemic	113
How to Survive a Plague	114
Irises	116
Somewhere Not Here	117
Black Moon	118
The Daisies	119
Wounded Deer	121
Sun & All	122

I

Girl in a Bee Dress

Still Life with Cheeses, Artichoke and Cherries

after Clara Peeters

Let them paint the fruits of commerce.
The heavy meats, the halved pomegranates,
the cornucopia
of olives and grapes from far-flung locales.
In some paintings
even the excess of exotic perishables
is lost in a sea of pewter, silver, gold.

Leave them to the Masters.
Better to lay out on the wooden table
cheese wheels in muted shades
and a single artichoke flowering on its plate.
At the center of display add no more
than a handful of cherries
to scatter a little color across the extravagant light.

Carousel

for Nadia Chomyn

The horses gallop, dance. prance
in and out of imagination.

Around the room, the sketched walls
ride up and down,
down and up
on the mind's carousel.

Silence an unexplored fairground—
a sky field
where colors run gladly together.

Trains wear ordinary lines,
travel to two-dimensional sounds
but the horses weave mystery harmonies,

speak merry motion language
that rises and falls.
falls and rises
like the sea rocking the sun to sleep.

Cottage Road

The name of the girl across the street
shone like copper. In the apartment below
a teen with a Mohawk
was already imagining the bomb
that would explode his hand into bloody petals.

When the leaves turned that year
the kids from the tenement
took turns jumping off the roof of an empty house
and called it flying.
I stood off to one side—
tried to explain the danger of broken things,
the treachery of glass.

The next day the boy with stitches
in a crooked line across his ass
would call me a witch
but that night the neighborhood stray
found its way up the stairs into my room—
its fur wild and warm against my face.
It was the beginning
of aloneness and of love.

The Dappled Horses of Pech-Merle

They gallop from one side of rock to the other
as if the possibility of wind and light

is real as the cave dwellers who painted them were.
Just one more leap, a final plunge

from interior into a dazzling unknown
and they're free. See the grasslands

opening before them as the prehistoric sun
beats down onto their spotted backs.

Far behind, the artists stand clumped in a group
at the mouth of darkness.

Their hands sign gestures to hold an emotion
there are no words for—the terrible, wonderful feeling

of watching a captured thing break away
from walls and become something entirely else,

an image that refuses to be tamed—wild
as any life that bucks the form it's been given

and shakes itself loose from shackles.

Girl in a Bee Dress

Whether the bees are arriving
or departing
is an unsolved mystery.
The pink daisy held with both hands
offers no information.

As for the girl, her eyes
are twin lakes that drown reflection.
The mouth stays silent too—
curves in no direction
as her body becomes a gown of wings
too dangerous to touch.

Maybe the shift away from innocence
is filled with venom.
On the other hand, what if the future
is beauty that hums electric
stings us only
when we fall back to sleep?

Bat Boy

The air streams past—
your feet pedaling fast, fast, faster
as the shapes of cars and houses
appear and dissolve
in the sharp, summer darkness.

You're the only kid on the street
but your mother doesn't stand in the doorway
and call out
into what to her looks like emptiness.

She knows you're not meant for rooms
sweltering with comfort—
can almost see
you pick up speed on the highest hill in town
black wings opening as you fall into flight,
the wide, wild soundwave world
spread out below you.

Poppy

> *If you take a flower in your hand and really look at it, it's your world for a moment.*
> —Georgia O'Keeffe

Forget the dark seeds at its core.

Instead hold out your hand.

Let heat fill the absence in your palm.

Let its flamenco petals catch

and flare across the gallery.

Ignore the couples wrapped

around each other so tightly

there's no air between them.

Ignore the way your aloneness

falls in upon itself like a star

collapsing or an old building

erasing its silhouette from sky.

The heart germinates unseen

and when it blooms, it flows

like a delicate, flickering sea.

Love is an unfolding.

American Primitive

Mid-August and already
on the lawn a maple leaf

crimson to its tips,
as if fall pressed its palm

against summer's green paper—
a handprint painting

that carries inside it
the blood of children

bullied in school yards
and shot in classrooms

or maybe only a pocketful
of secret Red Hot

hearts—the kind
that melt the lonely,

burn on the tongue.

Find

He would have been no more
than the size of a sparrow,
but no one knows the arc of his flight
or if his kind flew at all.
Even so, his chestnut fuzz caught the world
for a moment in its own amber, in an idea
of dinosaurs roaming the earth,
bounding blue and crimson and canary yellow
across uncharted possibilities—
each one trailing ten-foot feathers
monstrous enough to fill with dark ink
but hollow just the same,
as if we really could rewrite
the history of survival from scratch—
only this time in a softer octave,
a watercolor blur of patterns lifting
over the enormous, indelible cursive
of so many species
trampling toward extinction.

After a Storm

Pale gray sky, as if the day
was old painting,
its colors faded past fixing.

Or maybe it was just that the rain
had washed the light too many times.

Either way, the yellow kite
churned in the winter sea
and I could taste the salt on my lips,

feel the dark's long shadow
as my grandfather waded out past safety
to bring back what was mine.

On the beach
my coat flapped around my body
as someone's hat
skipped across the sand.

We never had a conversation
or went anywhere alone,
and I still wonder what it meant—

or if it meant anything at all—
that plunging into weather
after such a bright, fallen thing.

Flight

It wasn't that kind of goodbye.
There was no intention.

No suitcase, no note,
no bandanna tied to a stick.

The park glowed emerald green
and the enormous trees

stood round the bench,
cloaked in a shadowy circle.

Then the sky turned fairy-tale dark
with feathers and clouds.

The girl's father appeared
at the end of the path

and pushed open the gate
as the roses bared their thorns.

When he brought her back
her grandmother served her

three cookies on a silver plate
and her mother rapped her knuckles

seven times with a ruler
but even the power of mothers

and numbers couldn't
break the spell.

The story had begun.

At the Moulin Rouge

after Toulouse-Lautrec

The dancer wearing red tights kicks out a leg and lifts her skirts with slender arms. An upper-class woman watches the can-can from a distance, her gloved hands folded in front of her as prostitutes clap. She is draped in pink but her thoughts are as hidden as her dark hair under its flowery hat. Her widowed chaperone, a study in black silk, is more shadow than form. Around them, men in frock coats also stare at the dancer then look away, then back again, a tide of desire and disgust that ebbs and flows. Even Yeats is there. He leans on the bar, his head full of myth and Maud Gonne. In twenty years, he'll down the rest of his drink and slip into an alleyway to meet her at last. Lautrec will be long dead from sex and alcohol by then. He cursed his father the Count to the last, even as his defiance rolled off the bed into the undertaker's bowler. But a century later his dancer still kicks out her leg in a crowded, music-filled room. Her hair still flies away from her face and her tights are as red as any revolution.

A Maid at the New Yorker Cleans Room 3327

Pigeon feathers don't faze me.
Nor numbers.
Isn't three
just another name for God?
Tesla's no god, no devil either
only a man
born in a storm.
The others cross themselves at the threshold.
Avert their eyes
so he can't photograph their thoughts
and send them to the Martians.
Me, I just give him a nod,
go about my business
and leave him to his.
They say his electricity
leaks from every socket—
that it's important
to sweep the electrons off the floor,
tread lightly
so our shoes don't ignite.
I press my bare hands
against the walls—
imprint the energy
across my palms.
Nobody wants to live
in a prison of numbers
but sometimes I steal enough magic
to dress all the alley cats
in coats of fire.

13 Ways of Looking at an Allison

after The Breakfast Club

I.

As it turns out, I like the black shit.
Burned the blouse
and stomped the headband
to smithereens.
Folded the blue jacket
and left it on his doorstep.

II.

Reader, I ignored him.

III.

My purse overfloweth
with Atwood and Plath,
Oxblood lipstick and Kohl
eyeliner. Banshees
on my Walkman,
charcoal pencils
in a black leather case.

IV.

I braid my hair
with ravens,
stitch the wings of bats
inside the hem of my skirt.

V.

The ring on my belly
marks the beginning of many circles.

VI.

O athletic boys of America
why do you always dream of girls
pretty in pink?

VII.

A man and a woman are one.
A man and a man are one.
A woman and a woman are one.
A compulsive liar and a nymphomaniac and a raven
are one.
It's not rocket science.

VIII.

Rain keeps falling.
Rain keeps falling.

IX.

Dear John Hughes,
I don't accept the fact
that I've got to spend the rest of reality

walking off camera
as a version of who you think
the average Foreigner fan
wants me to be.

X.

On Wednesdays I wear
white.

XI.

I rode cross country
on a '67 Harley.
A man in a station wagon
mistook my shadow
for a bitch
on a broomstick.

XII.

The desert moon arcs across the sky.
My heart
must finally be undying.

XIII.

It's been night all night.
Would you recognize me?
I'm not of Simple Minds
but I'm dancing
you know it, baby.

Hey, hey, hey, hey

Ghost

He treated her with personal violence.
—from a petition to pardon Frankie Silver
 after she murdered her husband with an axe, 1833

All day they gathered by the river.
The conjure man with the gun to his head
shaking at the edge of water,
his glass globe small on a string.

They forgot the cold and the wind.
Fear or maybe excitement
pushing them forward up the hill
toward discovery, the bones

charred beneath the floorboards,
the heel of a boot barely covered
by a heap of ash. Even the man
himself looked surprised,

as if he hadn't understood
what truth looked like,
had never seen death's right form.
Life broken into pieces,

everything that was ever good
between us stained ugly.
The cuffs clanked round my wrists
as we went and the pines

whispered lullabies, over and over,
hushing my mind's roar, but the blue
distance said nothing
and the sky passed no judgment.

They buried him three times
in the cemetery. The markers
fade side by side—the evil
incremental, multiplied

every time I remember how
he smashed his fist into my face.
The baby quiet in a corner,
too scared for sound.

It was always me who cried,
the darkness in me hungry,
unsoothed. I always thought
it was love that bloomed black

in the cabin—love's hot, sweet
petals opening in silence after hurt.
The truth is you can't conjure real.
At night I hold its shape up

against the moon but every time
I glimpse its face the light
shifts, the mirror in me veiled,
a river minus stars.

The Dream Pilot

All the unreal moments scatter across the beach.

They fade and flame like trick birthday candles or moonlight's shimmery detritus. White light bounces off everything tangible— shells and broken glass, sand and water, seaweed, the sound of waves, a dark puzzle of rocks.

If I close my eyes, the radiance diamonding sea is still blinding. Ghost fire haunts my skin and hair, dapples the colors I've collected in my bucket of fantasies. Reality's sticky, uncomfortable as a wet bathing suit, the kind of grit that won't wash off.

I don't know if I'm a coward or not. I don't know what you'd say if I asked because I never ask. I'm fluent in the language of fear, can shutter my mind against love in a single bound, wrap moth wings in wool for safekeeping.

Don't get me wrong. Tomorrow I'll walk tightropes with strings of hearts tied round my ankles, write your name in circles across the blue, blue air.

Photographic Survey, 1919

The town a secret inside a forest—
trees overgrown on streets,
shops disappearing into dust,
the medieval cloaked in silence.

From that height there were no birds,
no graves, no bones to tell
how plague came calling and erased every name—
how it hid even the place itself away
for centuries.

From that height sunlight fell golden
onto my wings and all the lakes shimmered
like polished shields.

There should be a word for it—
the seconds before a man finds what's been
lost for so long. The seconds after.
The shift inside.

I remember her eyes, the scent of hay,
of skin, The glare at my back.
Me whispering to her in a voice
she didn't remember, her lips answering
in a language she did.

Monet at the Louvre

While others set their easels before Old Masters
and copied the fall of shadow across fruit
you moved yours to a window
to sketch riffs on clouds,
the swish of women's skirts,
a line of carriages, restless horses.

Even at 17, you never tired of the way the light
ebbed before surging back onto the canvas
again and again—as if anyone at all
could catch the simple genius of the sun.

The Scars

tell a story of steel and heat,
of nights spent feeding hungry ovens—
my left arm a poem written in reds.

Like all hot, bright things
the scars flare and fade.
I could name them but don't,
these small flames that brand me as working class—
warn the wealthy I might be the type of girl
who sings demon songs.

In the mornings the sun
slants through the windows
and signs its name across the hurt.
Fire always finds its own.

Wherever you are
roll up your sleeve and speak to me
in the language of burn.
Let us learn each other's radical cadences.
Let us watch our little anarchies ignite.

Breathing Lessons

Saturday at the city pool,
swimsuits splattered across blue canvas—
Jackson Pollock
of color and translucence.

I tell her the water
will catch her.
I tell her she's got to let herself
fall headlong into fear.

Eyes screwed shut,
arms out, face down—
the line where sky meets azure
blurred to light on skin.

Across the air
a boy flings graffiti onto silence.
My daughter takes a breath
and plunges into risk.

II

Fierce Mythologies

Revolution in the Back Bay

I want to fall with you out of loosestrife vernacular
into words resembling intimacy
out of dream into bread
out of fucking into salt
out of love into taste.

Say yes off the cuff.
Say yes to no.
Think or don't think
as long as you stand beside me
when I tear the heads off the roses
and scatter the red across polished floors.

Let the maître d' come running.
Let the married man stare.
Let his mistress look away as her glass
slides off the table into pieces.

I'm warning you now—
escape by candlelight involves a flock of napkins
and a pinch of pepper thrown over the wrong shoulder.

Take my hand.
Let running become us.
Let night fling open all its doors.

Fourth of July

The harbor is stars and stripes
and too many ferries
painted to look like fish.

Every last one is stuffed to the gills
with tourists.
They file down the docks
armed with cell phones and sippy cups,
strollers, sunblock, diaper bags
and conversations easily overheard.

We're tourists too, whether or not
we admit it. The view from deck
is a skyline we should have dreamed as kids
but didn't.

So when the sun flings its light at water
and the surface webs into a thousand mirrors
a feeling we can't count on
flickers into being.

When it's all over the sails of the boats
fill with shadows and the winds inside us—
flagless and firespun—
billow out across what we tell ourselves
is the obvious world.

Transport

after Robert Desnos

In the cafes when you woke out of a trance
the wine trembled in crystal glasses
and even the wintery light stopped to listen,
your voice a wave cresting over noise.

Back then, surrealism smelled like leaves
and cigarettes and willowy girls
whose gowns shimmered piano keys.
Back then, you couldn't stop for logic

or just plain sense—the world
an iceberg melting in a desert, its hot
jazz seas fanning out across monotony.
It wasn't until Auschwitz that you really

got it though. Knew that to read happy lives
in the sea of palms held open before you
was to be, for an hour, immortal—
the guards confused, unsettled,

even a little afraid as they loaded
so many skeletons back onto the truck
and drove away from death
while awaiting further orders.

American Girls

At the soda fountain, a row of girls and dolls
with combed hair and clear eyes
sip pink frappes from pink straws,
their perfect pink lips mining sweetness.

We stand a little apart, doll-less
and spent after a day of school shopping.
It's hard not to touch things.
The endless outfits and boxes of bitty babies,

the flip-flop rainbows and the sleds
complete with matching dogs. Above us,
mothers wait while their daughters
stand by their charges, watching silently

as scissors trim bangs and clip
stray curls. Further from reality,
attendants paint miniature decals
on pastel nails and apply sticky lip gloss.

Further still, a nervous child
fills out an admissions form
as her look-alike on crutches
dozes in a distant chair.

I suppose we'll never know
how it feels to play at any life we want—
fantasy safe inside affluence's glass—
but it doesn't matter.

We embrace the rumpled air as we step out again
into the fine, flawed world.

Before Further Testing

The dog sits on the edge of the bed,
watching what looks to me like silence
after snow, the gleam of yard
muted by clouds.

There's more to it than that,
of course, but for once my limitations
make me glad. I'm not ready
for the countless things
hidden beneath the dusting of calm
that's settled onto the woods.

Last year he brought me starfish
from our Christmas tree
and laid them at my feet,
as if I were a goddess meant to weave
her own constellations
or maybe just a mermaid
stranded in a dry land.

Now he brings me nothing
but it doesn't matter. It's enough
to be here—safe in the space
between knowing and not knowing.

Beneath the snow field of my skin,
galaxies of cells
are stringing fierce mythologies
through the branches of my body.
What animal can catch its dark constellations
and lay them before me?

Cancer Center: Key

1. River

Two brothers crammed into a single wheelchair,
one sick, one well,
play video games in safe anonymous silence.

An old couple shares a newspaper
casual in their closeness.

2. Building

A wall of glass stretches from one end of waiting to the other.

The size of boredom
fits like a window.

3. Bridge

A man kneels toward Mecca
as a woman lays her head onto the backside of faith
and sobs.

4. Overpass

A diseased heart makes its own arteries.

5. Tunnel

The girl in the elevator clings to a toy
a little too young for her—

disappears behind closed doors.

6. Orchard

The hat tree in the wig shop
leafs into hope,
        flowers pink and blue buds
the size of hands.

Dragon

Some days the fire in me
flickers out, darkness a kingdom
I don't want to visit.

My mind's a cave of weak light,
muffled weather. From the shadows
my mother's bones
gleam her violent goodbye
but I still don't know what wakes it—
this thing inside me
that heaps rage onto a pyre
and makes destruction blaze.

I still don't know why
when it's over I slink back to safety—
stolen swords and chain mail
stuffed under my wings,
my belly bloated with blood
I don't need. At night I polish the silver
until the useless shines.

In every spoon I see myself—
scales that glow green as envy,
body turned small and upside down.

Radium Girls

Everything glowed, inside and out,
Our faces, fingernails, shoes.
At night our dresses whirled across the dance floor
in haunted, dizzy circles
but by day the numbers on the watch dials
didn't move
and even the clocks on the factory walls
hung almost motionless.

The sun that slanted through the windows
was laced with ghost dust
as our brushes traced the same luminous circumferences,
over and over. *Lip, dip, paint.*

Such delicate hands, he said as he leaned over me,
though whether he meant mine
or the ones arabesquing at six and two
I couldn't say.
Later, when my jaw came away from my skull
I imagined his kiss
pressing all the way through the skin of my palm
to the shine beneath.

The girl on the other side of beginning
died last week.
I wasn't there and I don't know about God,
but the scientist who wrote the book
explained that the sign of Radium is Ra,
atomic number 88,
an infinity that doubles and doubles
until it reaches the bright edges of the human mind.

It was not much comfort.
Better to be our own absences—
weightless inside our fiery honeycombed bones
as we dissolve into a painless light.

What the World Really Feels Like

Coke cans and refrigerator doors
are wired with needles.
Even the clip on the dog's leash
has an electrical storm hidden beneath
its cool exterior.

All week, there's chemo fire in ice.
It burns in my mouth—flames
licking my insides on the way down
to the center of hell.

I almost like it—to reach for a spoon
and grasp the heat that pulses
through such a small, unassuming thing—
or to step outside in winter
and press my fingertips
against the air's fierce windows.

Some mornings I hold a pitcher of water
up to the light
just to remind myself
that even what's most beautiful in this world
can fall like glass through us all.

Pygmalion 2.0

She looks good bald.
She's never bitchy before coffee.
She can recite both definitions for crow's feet
though her silicone is smooth as the skin
of a girl on the brink of beauty.
She knows the names of every extinct bird
and can finish your codes for you.
She likes threesomes.
She never says no.
She never corrects your algorithms.
Her perfect body
bends in any direction
and her delicate sense of smell
can be calibrated
for every contingency.
At night under the neon moon
she curls herself inside your embrace
to whisper that she loves you.
You close your eyes
and as you dissolve in the taste
of those plump spun-sugar binaries
you almost believe it.

Nightmare

Your voice flickers in silence
like light slanting down
through fathoms of sleep.
In bare feet and a Batman t-shirt

you fight your way out of emptiness,
stumble toward the familiar.
Your mind lags behind, still dreaming
dark places. The dog raises his head

but whether it's the sound of fear
that rouses him or the jangle of words
I've tossed at you all at once, I'm not sure.
In the end you settle for a hug

that doesn't really do much of anything—
pad back across the hallway
to the cave of aloofness
all teen-agers live in.

Come morning we'll resurrect the argument
about angel wing tattoos and chicken-pox
piercings in unacceptable places.
But for now time's small

as a newborn's grasp. I can hold
the distance between your first and last cry
between the whisper of breathing,
the beat of a pulse.

The Cloud Sisters

after Maggie Taylor

One in green, one in blue, they sit
side by side on air or possibly a bench
hidden behind vision.

It isn't easy, wearing the weather for so long—
smiling frozen smiles
while clouds float by in gauzy disarray
and rain scatters seeds of clarity
between silken folds.

One dreams her body leafing out into spring,
feels her limbs unravel in earth
as her head reaches light's ceiling—
becomes petal and wind.

The other never sleeps, only writes
and rewrites the darkest corners of sky,
the endless churning sea.

Urban Decay as Latex Paint Color Palette

What I'm afraid to call my office
smells like paint samples.
The walls flicker possibilities I could dwell in—
Rapture Red and *Ruby Ring*,
Tropical Sea and *Azure Tide*,
Sunset Drive, Big Sky, Firenze.

Each square gleams like a shade snapped at dawn,
as if there's nothing easier—
just a little tug
to invent another future.

In town, the mills hulk in darkness.
Their broken windows glitter in the cold,
illuminating a universe
of vape shops and nail salons and liquor stores,
pizza parlors and weed dispensaries and empty storefronts.

I wonder what color the marketers in their cubicles
would name decay.
Would they say the bricks glow like *Phoenix Fire?*
Call the acres of vacant lots
Primeval Forest?

Castle Rock

The girls swim in silver, their pale slippers
skimming the mirror's surface.

The studio is a trail of tiny leaps and turns
that ripple out across reflection
and dissolve into memory.

In the hallway, mothers crowd the window
to watch strangers film a show you can stream
on Hulu. It's a story about evil,
about what depravity will do to you if you let it
or even if you don't.

A man aims his camera at a church that looms
over everything, and I think of a former student
who broke into a house in town
to murder an old woman in a wheelchair.

After she killed her
she called her mother and left a message.
Hi, mamma, I love you.

We always want to see what's darkest.
Did the heroin in her veins bloom black leaves that night
as its monster tar
spread through every branch of her body?

Or did she carry death with her all along—
undetected in the pocket of a Disney backpack,
hidden on the sole of a soft pink shoe?

Closed & Open Spaces

Early sunlight fires the snow
until the world is pure glare—
as if there's nothing left of landscape
but the future, the whole yard
an endless blank page
I'm not sure I'll be able to fill.

The dog hovers by the door,
half delirious with impatience,
but I ignore him and turn instead
to the cobalt plates in the dishwasher,
the waxy green ivy
tumbling over the counter.

Through the archway the oak table
leans, as always, to one side
and the raw silk curtains
reflect a glassy shade of sea.
I pour coffee into a mug and add creamer
until it's richly brown.
On days like this, only the intimacy
of things can rescue me.
Everything immense
can wait a little longer.

Names

The boxes on the front step
are addressed to a street number
that doesn't exist. Next door
too many cars snake down the driveway.
I don't know if something terrible happened
and I don't know if *Johanna Kozlowski—*
who went shopping online
and typed in the wrong address—
lives there or not. Just like I don't know
what makes the real [insert celebrity name here] real
and whether tweets
called in to an assistant to an assistant
get garbled along the way like stories at parties.

Here's what I do know: I know at the hospital
every hundredth time the nurse asks me
to confirm my name
I want to tell her the number of women
who pass themselves off as cancer patients
is probably nil. I want to tell her
I'd be more than happy to slip out of my name
the way I let my coat fall from my shoulders,
the way I kick off my shoes
at the end of a long day.

But I want to tell her this, too—
that if I did I'd set my name aside
on the back of a chair, at the front of a closet,
so I could put it on again if I needed to.
That maybe that's all anybody really wants—
to know in some corner of sky
God or somebody else of equal authority
is standing just out sight,
holding the threadbare robe
that passes for their fucked-up life.

That it's never too late.
That what looks like holes in the sky
will always be stars.

Blue Nude

after Henri Matisse

After the sculpture shattered
you decided to paint it

in light as hard as the floor
that refused to spare her—
to brush reality in broad, dark strokes.

Big feet, thick brows, and biceps
strong enough to wrestle
any sailor's arm to the table.

Maybe you wanted to take
all the fragility out of art,
to repair the cracked places in yourself.

Or maybe you wanted to translate
what the clay said as you knelt
to cup its broken breasts:

that every body is carved from the same form
that once scuttled across ocean floors.

Surveillance Capitalism as Lady's Companion

Forget the cat sprawled across the floor,
its fur bright in the spangled sun.

Forget the knitters, the nodders,
the genteel holders of hands.

Forget the Friend that remembers birthdays
and replies to texts
in a language of indecipherable emojis.

How much easier to employ the algorithm ready
inside the computer, the ghost in the phone.

Attuned to your every impulse, she advises *blonde*
when you search *red*

summons *lingerie* when you whisper *lonely,*
diagnoses *major depressive disorder*
when you think *sad.*

And why not?
Who else can kaleidoscope your darkest secrets
into luminous stained-screen patterns?

She's even calculated the cost of the life
you don't know yet you (don't) want.

Don't delay. Act now.
Suggestions are never running out.

Portrait of a Lady

My head a cloud

        of feathers and flowers,

I emerge

                a doll descending a staircase,

layer upon layer

        of beauties piled on.

All so I can cross an avenue

                traverse a park

                        ignore the nannies.

            It took so long

to learn to walk in air,

            to know the weight

        of birdsong gone silent

                            artificial roses

ribbons bent into bows

I'm a walking vase, a study in baroque—

                slightly less

well behaved than the chandelier above me,

        the one that trembles

                                    at every man's approach.

It's true: an army of hatpins

                    presses into my scalp

but my hair's a nest in which dark things hatch

                            and my gloved left hand

        is only a motion away from dangerous.

Signs in Winter

The test comes back better
than expected.

Outside, the wind whirls dead leaves
and knocks branches
onto patches of melting snow.

Almost fifty degrees in January!
So warm
it's hard not to believe that tomorrow the air
will arrive bearing the scent of lilacs,

that the stingy sun
will scatter long days filled with light
across the garden path.

Pigeons

In the afternoons when the bus dropped us at our stop, they were always there. Day after day they drew invisible circles across the sky—as much of a constant as our math teacher scratching geometry onto the blackboard, though the birds' math was more beautiful. At dusk, the pigeons dove through tangled shadows and disappeared inside our neighbor's coops for the night. Most were grayish blue, or maybe bluish gray, with dark bands across their wings and iridescent necks. They never landed any place but the coops and at night they were too far off for my brothers and I to hear them cooing. There were dozens of them and the air glowed like canyon walls as they swooped down through layers of sunset.

When I went back the coops stood vacant and the paint had chipped away. I asked around and found out that the man who raised them for decades had died. It was only then that I realized I knew almost nothing about him. Not where he worked or how he had died. Not what his favorite food was or what TV shows he watched or if he loved his wife. He may as well have been an axe murderer for all the attention us kids had paid him when we lived in the neighborhood. His grown-up children swooped in from out of town to sell the house and then flew out again before anybody had the chance to read his obituary. But the idea of the pigeons was strangely persistent. I kept remembering the way they circled the neighborhood like silent sentinels keeping us from scattering. As if that loopy childhood cursive still held us inside it.

Once when I was in Venice I ran full speed at a crowd of pigeons just to watch them rise and fall back into place. They were overfed and the sheen of their feathers seemed too dull for flight but I sat on a bench and studied them anyway. They scratched hieroglyphics across the piazza as the tourists rushed past and I went on sitting there, thinking about the past. That was before I understood you can drown in stone and sky as easily as in water.

Before I learned survival is mostly about forgetting. Even so, I like to imagine my neighbor's pigeons from time to time—I keep trying to decipher the messages. And I can't help wondering if anybody will do the same for me.

Black Dog

My feet go numb at the halfway mark
and darkness seeps into the cold,
blotting houses and trees
and the shapes of distant cars.

The dog tugs on his leash, oblivious
to doctor's orders to take things slow.
Every now and then, pain or maybe fear
flickers and fades, making me glad
for once that neither of us
knows a thing about moderation.

At a bend in the road, a black dog
barks at us but stays where he is
and it's hard not to turn him
into something he's not—a warning
heeded in the nick of time, a reprieve.

Yellow light spills out of windows
and suddenly it's good
to be on the other side of warmth—
here in the wintery night
where it's impossible to tell the difference
between the present
and a century ago and a dream.

In its corner of sky, the moon rises
frail and ghostlike and distant
as tendrils of smoke
uncurl from nearby chimneys.

III

Peace Roses

Rose-Colored Sunglasses

You are going to ask: and where are the lilacs?
—Pablo Neruda

As it turns out, changing the world
is cheap. Five bucks for a reality
soft as strawberry ice cream,

where all wings shine like the feathers
of flamingoes and every flower
breathes dawn's watercolor dance.

Don't speak to me about death.
In their coffins, the children's
cheeks are ruddy with health

and the babies sleep in cradles
stained a variation on spun sugar.
At night, darkness intercedes

but that's okay. There's freedom
in an unlit room, in the mind
at rest with its shade pulled down.

In the morning if the alarm
wakes me too soon,
weave songbirds through my hair

and fill your arms with cherry blossoms.
Let your lips brand sonnets
across my body and keep springtime

by the bed. Expect the broken
to appear in dreams
without warning. Be vigilant.

The Unusual Suspects

Virginia Zoo Not Giving Up in Search for Missing Red Panda
—WAVY-TV

A ringed tail eclipses an edge of roof.

Cinnamon fur flickers inside a trash can.

A kitten's mask floats underneath a porch.

Meanwhile, zookeepers with thermal cameras

roam lawns in search of sources of heat,

postmen keep watch while delivering mail,

raccoons scurry down unlit alleyways

and a fox whose coat falls inside the spectrum

between autumn leaves and a sky redder than blood

cloaks its brightness with thickets of shadows.

The City

is frozen but it never stops just goes
on as in on the street outside our hotel
with the mermaid-themed décor a woman
is walking her dog and in the bakery
behind glass the strawberry-glazed cakes
keep on shining like mad and at Rockefeller
Center wall-to-wall tourists turn and turn
to gawk at the Christmas tree just like
they've been doing for a million years
its lights colored small stars smaller
than we expected its shape a bell
drowned by buildings and combat-gear
guards but still still still there's something
here a kind of motion I want to take with us
all the way back up North on the dark
cold ride to Massachusetts where I'll set life
on a shelf and watch as it pulls fine
fiery dust out of the late afternoon air.

Cancer Center

Almost everyone in the cafeteria
is some version of sick.
Women with bright, patterned
scarves wrapped around their heads,
children whose huge, dark eyes
make their faces seem
almost translucent,
old men lost inside their clothes.
Even the mothers
who lift trays and pour juice
look as if their tiredness
penetrates to the bone.
Here and there, nurses
exchange gossip over coffee
and a doctor eats quickly
without looking up
before rushing through
bright antiseptic corridors
to save someone's life
or tell someone else
it's too late for anything
besides mercy.

Prelude

Lately I wear sanity close to my skin.
Thin as a slip
it could slide over my bones at any moment,
pool at my feet.

The world's gaslighting us all.
Surreal flickers its endless feed—
dystopia a slow seduction.

At work last week a guy stood up
and slashed a knife down his screen.
When he walked by on his way out
no one understood
or maybe everyone understood.

Outside wind rattles the panes
and night sweeps across suburbia.
The tick of the clock is a metronome—
the footfall of the end of things,
America's timebomb heart.

Wintering

To wrap ourselves in red suddenly
seems essential. Not as heat,
sirens, five-alarm fantasies—
I don't want seduction
slinking around my mind,
draping appeal over a drop-dead body.

In summer it didn't matter
or maybe I didn't notice
the blank at the center of the table
where roses would have
bloomed. Somehow I missed
the missing words
between dawn and sundown.

Back then the space seemed harmless
as a kid's gap-toothed smile
but now I need to fill every drawer
with ruby sweaters,
set wool socks ablaze.

I want to pour us each a glass
of the old love whiskey—
because maybe it's not too late
to remember its banked-fire burn.

The Blue Tree

shines through the window
each branch weighted with a universe
of discount-store stars.
In all honesty, it's nothing
like that other year—
me barreling home
after another bad day armed with box
upon box of red string lights,
their demon eyes
scaring off the neighbors
and alarming the dog.
No, this year's something wholly
different, the tree more
than a riff on sky, lake, sea—
its shape a bell rippling
from some unseen center.
Witness the color of serenity
burning steady in darkness.
Note how the tree holds itself absolutely
still at the eye of blue,
how it waits
for even the recycled tinsel
to free itself from cliché and gleam
in the room's snow-globe silence.

Peace Roses

When the Nazi invasion of France seemed imminent, Francis Meilland sent eyes of the plant to rose growers that he knew in Turkey, Germany, Italy, and the United States.
—Connie Crochmal

The vase on the table's a fallen chandelier—
a miniature universe
where yellow suns electrify the night.

In the silence I hear them humming bees' jazz.
They're in constant dialogue with the refrigerator,
the light above the stove,
the brash orange chair
stashed in the attic.

My mind is a hive,
alive with syrupy dreams
but the taste of ash burns my tongue.

I can feel the darkness woven with beauty—
see the hungry ghosts
forced to march to the tune of Hitler's Taps
on the day a rose grower set out for his fields
to save a handful of buds
before the Nazis arrived.

You can break a magnet in half,
but you can't snap its opposites.
Good and evil bound by stardust and blood—
Death's dark blanket in the same crib
as the innocence
that sleeps in every newborn.

Dear Lamp

in a room I've never
seen—cold as walls,
sharp as corners—
shine your yellow
sun bulb into folds
between curtains,
along spaces under
doors. Bestow
without elegance
your sturdy, factory-
grown glow, your
sensible radiance,
and if you can manage
it in those darkest hour-
glass moments
before dawn,
scatter every last
brightness across
all the unswept webs,
the silent insomniac night.

Dear Egg

dear birdsong
singer of
chalkboard
scraping unsongs
dear anonymous
whose abbreviated
unwords crack
the ugly open
again and again
just to watch
it run yellow
down faces
dear whoever
you aren't
for one sweet
burst of silence
hesitate
before splintering
into pieces
the shell that
holds this frail
boned world
inside it

Color in February

This morning the curtains glow
the color of embers.
Don't get me wrong. It's still winter,
still New England
and on the other side of the window
the mute trees hold the cold inside them.

If I step outside for five seconds
it will settle into me too
but this morning, propped up in bed,
engulfed by aquamarine pillows
and honeyed shadows
I could be in Florida or Morocco.

Even if I'm not, the sun is getting stronger
by the minute. Soon enough
there will be places in the body
the cold won't reach.

Palmyra

Beyond all these wonderful ruins extends an ocean of blazing sand, stretching all the way back to the horizon that appears to shimmer like a blue sea
—Louis-Francois Cassas, 1785

Strange, how there are places
where worlds meet.
Sand becomes sea becomes
sky, the line between
earth and air, past
and present, wavering
like a curtain filled with fire.
A rebel hides among
the ruins, machine gun
heavy against his shoulder,
the blood of an infant
smeared across his shirt.
Behind the clouds
the drone of a plane
splits silence in two
just as empires earlier
the march of Aurelian's
troops on their way
to burn the city to ash
echoed through the temples
and the market square,
set a sleeping child crying.

In Defense of Partiality

You can see right off he's not the kind of cat
meant for windows
yet there he sits in perfect stillness,
as if so much time spent behind glass
has siphoned all the motion out of his life.

As morning crowds blur by
his rain-smeared reflection
settles a little more each week.

There are more important losses to be sad about—
bombs leveling cities,
children starved inside their skins,
the kind of pain that courses through the body
and stops the heart.

Every moment is full of lists
too long to memorize,
but here, on this day, grant me
this small grief
for a living thing trapped too long.

On the Drive Home

The rain lets loose and a storm
rips the sky over Albany.
The air is anything but delicate,
just clouds torn to pieces
and stars flung into another
view—constellations
falling out of formation
like pearls dropping
off a broken necklace.

Miles behind me, you unpack
coffee maker and string lights,
arrange black pillows across your bed—
your roommate a profile
who owns a minifridge
and intends to study Portuguese.

Tomorrow I'll open all the windows
and hope for the best.
Maybe the wind
will come and sweep away the quiet.
Maybe the roses in the garden
will hive the sun
and your absence
will taste of amber.

If not, I have plans
to paint your room red
or possibly green—find out
if what my doctor said is true—
that if it must the heart
can make its own arteries.

Terra Incognita

Sometimes the words
step off the page
and you can see all the way
to the edge of knowing.

The images turn clear
as air in winter
and the sky reels
toward a dark you can't name.

That's when you notice
the idea aglow
at the end of the mind.
Its yellow windows

shine such beauty
you set out on a journey
that might change your life,
might not.

Glassmaker's Travel Diary

after Leopold Blaschka

Grief doesn't bloom/doesn't float but falls/shedding
stillness until it touches black/the ship motionless
on a mirror sea/becalmed a word for a state of mind
that might mean trapped/might mean caught in
an absence of wind/yellow fever took my wife/
my father dead too/America an idea on the other
side of waiting/at night the sea creatures rise up
onto my sketch pad/swim across my eyelids/when
I get back I'll turn them into light/dip memory
in melted sand/memory a word that should
mean forever but doesn't/the color of her eyes
wavers/the shade of her hair in summer/my father
wearing a suit and folded arms/becomes watercolor/
his voice lost in breaking waves/the jellyfish glow
translucent as they disappear/when I get back
I won't let them go/because replica is a word for
a state of being so strange/it can live at depths
where mortality is only a loose net of syllables.

Poet vs. Novelist

The rain's been tapping on the roof
all day, the sound steady
as an author beginning a new book.

If I want to, I can read the drops
that fan out across the window
in row after translucent row.

Instead I'm thinking about the little bottle
on the sill, how its green glass
holds so many beads of air caught in stillness.

Star Trek Power Ballad

after Edgar Mitchell

The astronaut dreamt flocks of doves
rising from moondust—wrote in his diary
that the only agenda aliens really have
is for us to get our shit together.

Meanwhile, new planets are waiting for us
to name them. They aren't like Pluto,
which tried to pass itself off as
part of our system
so we'd put its photo in textbooks.

So what if on a few of them
day and night live perpetually divided?
Who cares if their star is colder and dimmer
than the one we've got now?

Because it's important not to lose
sight of the main idea. To know we're ready
for any catastrophe—
that if we can just fly a little faster
we can set out for new worlds to wear out.

Blue Jays

I don't know why they stay.

The bike at the edge of a neighbor's yard
has rusted into a memory
buried beneath the snow

and off in a far corner
an orphaned swimming pool ladder
sinks to one side
like a suburban Tower of Pisa.

It's one of those days
when the world seems used up
but there they are again,
flickering from tree to tree.

Their wings fan out across the gloom
as if to remind me
what the sky is capable of.
They're that blue.

It's been winter all winter
but if anybody asks
I'll tell them the light

that travels years to get here
is on its way
is on its way.

Garden Path with Chickens

after Gustav Klimt

One's stopped mid-way to stare
at something inside the colors.
The other, at least partly on task,
is almost there. There being,
as always, a place too shadowed by distance
to describe in much detail.

That's the thing with beauty.
Some days it can reach out from the sidelines
and stumble you cold.
If you're not vigilant it just might turn you
away from forward for good.

Truth be told, even chicken number one
never reached his place in the shade—
the painting hidden in the Austrian castle
torched by SS troops
on their march toward history.

Witness hollyhocks, morning glory.
Witness the painting, the leaves,
the sun that some fine century
will surely burn
even its own light to the quick.

The Skirt

hangs on the end of the rack
its green silk
swaying
in an artificial breeze.
It's nothing like the sea
but I think of
the sea anyway—
its coolness and its waves
edging ever closer
to shore
then emptying all the pearls
from its pockets
before disappearing
into depths where no one
can follow.

Red Barn in Snow

It's simple things that take the most space.
Sea and sky, childhood's watercolor summers,
Land, silence, loneliness, wind.

At the center of the field, the red barn
weathers another snowstorm.
Its faded exterior speaks of lean years,
accumulated losses.

It sits where it always has, not far
from trees rooted in immensity.
And I don't think it matters
if I tell you what type of trees they are,
or the names of the dead
who thought they owned them—

but I can't stand here and not be sure
we'll find our way back
to everything we believed about love.

IV

Two Mirrors

Tulip Fever

The heavy clouds churn, steeped in gray
but there are more walkers out than usual.
Some wear masks, some don't,
depending on whether they want space
or conversation.

All along the street, daffodils bloom in bright,
neat clusters, but their cheery insistence on Spring
doesn't move me.
I prefer the black dog with the over-sized ears,
the one whose eyes give nothing away.

If there were tulips, it might be different.
Not the usual variety found in gardens or along
front walks. Red, yellow, white.
Solid, reliable colors that endure year after year,
their survival never in doubt.

No, I want the ones the Dutch Masters
would pay a year's salary for,
outrageously gorgeous in their excess.
Sometimes madness makes sense.
In Amsterdam, 1637, a single tulip bulb

would sell for more than a mansion—
the place infected with a fever for broken flowers.
The most valuable
marked by an anomaly
that split petals into ragged streaks of crimson, gold, purple.

Of course, they didn't know it was sickness
that caused the colors to climb so brightly upward
devouring as they undid the ordinary
and killed planned fields
the wealthy had already paid for.

Maybe it is a story about folly, or greed,
but I like to tell myself
it was something more—
that the city understood in a sudden, constant way
beauty is a burning thing.

Future Shock

Barns flare at regular intervals
        as if somebody stitched color
onto summer's green blanket

but it's the sign that stops us—
        paint faded beyond brightness
and only the one word, *Cocktails,*

hanging off-kilter on a ghost motel
        at the dead center of abandoned.
For a curve of time, the laughter

of women wearing cat's-eye sunglasses
        and sleeveless dresses drifts
toward men who drink their martinis

straight up. We can't decide if anybody's
        life was ever that easy,
just like we don't know if America

was ever great. Before we come to
        anything resembling insight
a bend in the road settles the place

into past until it becomes one more
        thread pulled out of *now*
and released into the partially pure air.

Up ahead, the sun rises, its blinding star
        burning at ten thousand degrees,
but whether we're driving into a beginning

or an ending is impossible to tell.

Post Chemo

Yesterday I dyed my hair.
Now I'm painting my toes.

I run my fingers through the flames
until the mirror catches fire.
I stare at my feet and watch poppies
bloom across linoleum.

Once, on the way home from a place
I don't remember
the road rose and went on rising.
It twisted and turned
and spun me too dizzy to think.

That's when the forest fell away
all at once
as I skidded toward the edge
of an unbroken blackness.

Sometimes it's easy to disappear.
Sometimes the beginning of disaster
curves out of nowhere.

When life flattened out again
I sipped coffee and skipped past familiar songs.
My almost death
dissolved behind me like a tip of ash
flicked out an open window.

This time around I want to leave
some trace. Nails hard and red as blood.
Color that imprints itself onto the retina.
Snatch of melody
that pops into your head at inconvenient times
and won't leave you alone.

Self Portrait as the Allegory of Painting

after Artemisia Gentileschi

Her arm extended, her sleeve
rolled up. In one hand she holds a brush,
in the other a palette, the canvas before her
a shade of brown
fallow as a field in November.

It took two mirrors to capture
the wild dark of hair pulled back,
the plain apron,
the dress with all its greens
gathering and evanescing.

But her reflection is no stand in
for art, or likeness, or vanity.
She knew it too.
Like Ripa did in his *Painting,*
she included a necklace
but left out
the medallion inscribed with the word *Imitation*
and she conveniently lost the cloth
tied over the woman's mouth.

Just what she's looking at, you can't know,
her eyes focused on what you can't detect,
at least not yet—
the image kept safe beyond sight,
a witness waiting to testify.

Museum of an Untrained Artist

The universe speaks in tongues. Above me, constellations shine ciphers I can't decode and here on earth, green notes fall from trees whose music I can't read. My grandfather translated the callings of birds into Audubon language—White-Throated Sparrow, Red Warbler, Yellow-Bellied Sap Sucker, Solitary Blue-Headed Vireo.

Back then, the distance between a Northern Red Oak and a Scarlet Oak could fill whole cartographies of difference. Even kids charted tides of wildflowers that spilled across back roads. Now forests are stepping out of their names. The labels trees once wore—Carolina Silverbell, Bearberry, Eastern Redbud—flicker like guttered candles.

My mind is an impressionism of twilight words. I keep at it though. Alive in the year's cage, I tape watercolor Rorschachs to concrete walls—tell myself it's not too late to turn imaginary fields into real windows.

At the American Philosophical Society
in the City of Brotherly Love

In this room of maps and glass
        cursive names roam
extensive meadows full of buffalo—
the old-world ink endlessly unfurling
its elegant, black flags
recording for fellow travelers
the long and barbarous names given these parts.

Conquest fades one word at a time.
So like a kind aunt
        I'll call death a long sleep
and assure you someday the earth will wake
to create its own cartography
as men once recorded the angles stars made
when they passed invisible lines.

Off US Highway 25, N.

The years wrap themselves around me.
My death lies curled inside
a tarpaulin chrysalis that fades
and fades under restless sky.
Above me, the seasons perch
on telephone wires,
flit across clouds as the air streams
through the dark hair of trees.
When snow fell the seventh year
and winter covered my body
I understood I had lost my name—
tried to climb ropes of syllables
until I remembered myself.
The sixteenth spring, I imagined
the creek beside me whispered
who I was but its words
floated downstream. On the thirtieth
I begged the dirt
to braid my story with oblivion.
How I want to dissolve.
How I want to dream these bones
fragile, flickering things
whose wings will catch, become flame.

Climate Cubism

The sky splits into a thousand riffs on inferno
as if Picasso's demon
painted the face of the world.

In Florida, alligators swim past sunken houses
but in California
the water has boiled off—

the land a kettle that sings volcano songs.
At the corner of the canvas a man pulls off a highway—
coaxes a rabbit to safety.

In this landscape of edges
to save one soft thing makes no difference
but sometimes it's necessary.

At the Solstice

The sun comes out all at once,
a sudden surge of light

blinding in its intensity.
Along the edge of the yard

the raspberry bushes
are weighted with rubies

and the flowers in the garden
bloom in bright disarray.

From behind sliding doors,
the dog watches and perhaps

wonders why the shaggy pines
can't shake off the darkness.

Chandeliers & Red Velvet

only a few stores apart. And it seems to me
that's what it all comes down to—spirit hived in glass

or the voluptuous. Behind its window a chandelier
prisms the moon into a thousand ghosts—

hall of broken mirrors diamonding the unseeable
into an idea of the thing inside that flickers,

won't be snuffed out. The neon sign down the block
has its own answer. Does it even matter

if I tell you the store is selling lingerie, sex toys,
or cupcakes rich with sweetness? If I remind you

what it's like to run your fingertips along the velvet
of desire? Maybe what matters is we're all searching

for the amalgam of two kinds of light—want
at the end of our darkness to locate the soul of heat.

Let us keep searching until we find it.
Let us burn a hole in the endless, silent sky.

Burning the Desk

I arrive late

    as memories not mine
                                      blaze

        and disappear in darkness.

I never knew her father as a child

            can only imagine

    an anonymous dark-haired boy

scratching away at homework

    and sheltering in place
                          in case of attack.

All at once an old drawer
                          ignites–

scatters sparks across moonless sky

                          and night becomes a prayer

at once ancient and alive.

        The Greeks got it right, I think.

Better to turn what's heaviest

        into constellations

that rise full of fire into weightless air

                              than walk this earth

                                        carrying our fathers'
bones.

Ritual

In July the dandelions glowed so hard
    they threatened to burn anything within reach.

Now they're almost invisible, the lawn
    a field of wishes tossed in wind.

I've let everything go. The grass bends
    toward the ground, the birdbath

that belonged to the owner before me
    rests in two pieces. All day I watch sparrows

imprint flight on sky and ignore the buzz of motors.
    At midnight I'll walk barefoot into darkness

and feel the flower ghosts rising up against my skin
    like the silvery dust of moonlight.

Learning to Knit During a Pandemic

The disease blooms numbers
that spread across maps and climb bar graphs.
In broad daylight they ride the wind,
dark petals drifting into the spaces between skyscrapers,
urban canyons
     no one visits.

Life turns inward. Coffee and books, dogs,
the sound of rain on the roof,
candles burning inside cheap, colored glass.
  I crave simple things,
locate yarn, needles, a video that promises
to teach me to knit in six easy steps.

Being left-handed, I suspect that, like everything in life,
the six steps won't be easy.
That the woman effortlessly weaving color into form
isn't telling all. There may be seven steps. Or eight.
But I go on.
Between my fingers crimson unravels
and remakes itself row by row, a stitch at a time,
clumsy as the beat
of a repurposed heart.

How to Survive a Plague

There are of course walls.
Sky high, boulder strong,
thick as the shadows of corpses
lengthening across a border.

But the circumference of any circle
isn't always enough.
It may be necessary to take
precautions—embrace

a radical vigilance. In Milan
for example citizens boarded up
houses from floor to rafters,
took note of the rapidity

with which flames could swallow
a family whole. If you prefer
there are islands steeped in sky—
places folded so snugly into distance

it's possible to sip tea, read books,
forget indefinitely the stench of bodies
curled back into innocence.
The choice is of course yours.

As for me, it's the cats I'll gather
as saviors. Just imagine
the bristle of orange electric fur,
the sweetness of tongues

licking bright bared teeth. Because
I think deep down everybody understands
the crazed feral comfort
of hunters. It's true though—

that sometimes at night in dreams, another madness, a fine
            feathered slip of sanity
cracks the world absolutely
                                              open—

carries us all for a blaze of moment into the wide
            wild spaces
that shift fantastically and so fucking
                                          beautifully

from red to gold to blue to black.

Irises

White Tiger. Bohemian Waxwing.
Night-blooming Cereus.
Even water, with its gift for shape-shifting
seemed like a metaphor
for some strange being I might become.

Blood work boring, CT scan unremarkable,
my oncologist tells me,
his voice cheerful over the phone
and I think of the airport—

remember the couple that streamed past
as I struggled slowly forward.
Their wheeled luggage trailed behind them
sleek and exotic.

But only for a moment.
On the back steps, the irises
my daughter picked up on clearance
slump over their cartons.

Their petals emit a papery, uncertain glow
like forgotten ghosts
lit at last by the Northern sun.

Somewhere Not Here

flocks of missiles lift in elegant curves
and the sky rains fire

onto a hut where a girl
pencils answers to problems

she can't solve. Somewhere not here
twins count each other's bones

as somewhere exactly like here
every forsythia bush blooms yellow

and the clouds go on tumbling across blue
in all their airy complexity.

Black Moon

When it's time, I set out lawn chairs
and pour champagne
into twin flutes that ring out when I tap them.
We'll sip summer one last time
as the moon disappears
for a second night this month.

They say there's nothing to see here—
that the B side of lunar
is always inferior,
absence just a sheet thrown over sky.

Maybe the realists are right.
Maybe the moon is as useless now
as a burnt-out bulb.
But this is also true: darkness is a room
waiting for form to emerge.

Tomorrow a sliver. By September
the light will hang so heavy in the night
that the trees will swell with fat, luminous fruit
and a pristine rain
will fall across the grass.

The Daisies

curve over the top of a green glass vase at the center of the oak table. I've cut the flowers too long so after four days they look translucent and gorgeously weary, like dancers in costume after a rehearsal. The sound of the occasional car drifts through the open windows. Further off, someone is mowing their lawn.

In the late summer light I sit down with a notebook and try to write out lists of tasks I've been thinking about for weeks. All the cleaning I have to do, the new job I need to find, the friends I should try to get back in touch with, the friends I've lost for good. I do my best to will my hand into writing out the new healthy diet I will follow and the contingency plans I should make, just in case things don't go the way the doctors hope.

Then there are the other lists, the ones that will include all the trips I'll take if I keep living and the love I'll find though I haven't found it yet and the novels I'll finish writing and the elaborate desserts I'll actually bake and the little black bikini I'll finally buy. It seems strange that it's summer, or maybe it seems strange that it's summer and I'm still here, in my house, at my table, sitting before an overfilled vase as cars full of people rush to wherever people rush to.

In December I lay in a wilted body at the center of a maze of tubes. To raise an arm or a leg took effort. To breathe took effort. On Christmas Eve I pushed myself out of bed, clinging to my IV pole as I maneuvered myself toward a row of regulation chairs at the end of the hospital floor.

Through the plate glass windows, far below, a Christmas tree shone in darkness, its needles clothed in a universe of LED lights. I'd like to say I imagined all the kids in their beds trying to fall asleep and all their parents assembling bikes incorrectly and all the other kids in other countries starving inside their skins and the terrible, unpredictable unfairness of the world.

I'd like to tell you I wondered about God. But the truth is I wasn't thinking about anything—just like I'm not thinking about anything as I sit here at my kitchen table six months later. The sunlight falls across the floor in wide squares. The ballerina daisies spill over the top of the vase. The wind streams through the windows and ruffles their ethereal skirts.

Wounded Deer

after Frida Kahlo

In the real world, she would already
be on her side, seconds away
from an indelible stillness.
But in the forest of the canvas
every defeated thing endures.
The ancient, hollow trees
branch into leaves—each tip
a brush waiting for whatever color
the artist chooses. Green, of course,
but also blue or red or the palest
gleam of brown—the shade
so many mistake for barren.
As for the deer, nine arrows
may as well be nine thousand.
Blink and she'll leap out of the image
into a painless intimacy with sky.
Close your eyes. Look. Can you
see our antlers snagging stars?
Feel the arrows along our spines
feathering into wings?

Sun & All

This morning the birds on wires
are writing power ballads.
As they scatter across the blue
each one adds a note
to the symphony of clouds and sky.

November's yellowed lawn
seems warmer in the rising sun
and even a neighbor's electric reindeer
are awash in impressionism.

I want to immerse life in a new language.
Make weather my personal metaphor.
Write a sonnet about radiance
and dedicate it to the ghosts of radical prodigals.

Sometimes I'm frayed around the edges
like the photo someone broken carries in their wallet
but only looks at in bars.
Sometimes I'm just about done.

Then light strikes against landscape
and a blaze of healing
burns away all the old ideas.
I close my eyes and count to three,
cross my fingers behind my back.

About the Author

Lori Lamothe is the author of three poetry collections, *Trace Elements* (Aldrich Press), *Happily* (Aldrich Press) and *Kirlian Effect* (FutureCycle Press), as well as several chapbooks, including *Ouija in Suburbia* (dancing girl press) and *Diary in Irregular Ink* (ELJ Press). Her work has appeared in *Blackbird, Calyx, Hayden's Ferry Review, The Literary Review, The Journal, The Seattle Review, Painted Bride Quarterly, Passages North, Third Coast, Verse Daily.* and elsewhere. A four-time Pushcart nominee, she lives in New England with her family and two rescue huskies.

www.ingramcontent.com/pod-product-compliance
Lightning Source LLC
Chambersburg PA
CBHW022014160426
43197CB00007B/430